SUMMARY OF THE BODY KEEPS THE SCORE

Mind, Brain And Body In The Transformation Of Trauma

Bessel Van der Kolk, M.D.

Effective Reads

Legal Note

Disclaimer

Important Information

In this summary, I will not focus on rewriting the book's content or copy-pasting the same table of contents. Instead, my goal is to provide you with a condensed version of the book's key insights. As a result, after reading through, you will understand everything you needed to know about the book.

Table of Contents

A Brief About Bessel Van der Kolk

Bessell Van der Kolk, MD, is a psychiatrist with extensive experience. He specializes in the field of post-traumatic stress and has written over 150 peer-reviewed scientific articles, most of which are about the subject.

Van der Kolk, a Dutchman, has indeed served as the president of the International Society for Traumatic Stress Studies. He has now become a psychiatry professor at Boston University School of Medicine.

Introduction

Van der Kolk, a psychiatrist and trauma expert, has written an unusual book titled The Body Keeps the Score. We are all aware of the psychological toll that psychological trauma may take on an individual's life. Trauma can hurt how people perceive themselves and the environment around them. Psychological trauma can have a long-term influence on the individual's loved ones as well as on the individual.

In this book, Van der Kolk delves into the complexities of how trauma creates these effects by taking a neuroscientific approach to the subject matter. Additionally, Van der Kolk discusses how neuroscience is allowing us to develop novel and effective treatments for psychological trauma sufferers.

Eye movement desensitization and reprocessing (EMDR), yoga, and limbic system treatment are examples of such approaches. Van der Kolk takes us on a tour of these cutting-edge treatments by recounting his own professional experience and the individuals he has treated. In that sense, this book can be thought of as a historical account of the mental health field over the last 30 years.

You will have a better understanding of how our brains react to and deal with psychological trauma when you have learned these. What Van der Kolk suggests is that survivors of psychological trauma receive assistance in their recovery.

Mental Health Care Is Ruined By Antidepressants

Van der Kolk explains how he and other researchers and therapists were overjoyed when antidepressants were first released into the marketplace. He now believes that our abuse of these pharmaceuticals has caused us to treat mental illness as if it were a disease, rather than a condition. Unfortunately, as a result of this strategy, the following elements of mental health support have been eliminated:

- The belief that we can cure one another in the same way that we can harm one another is a dangerous one.

- Our ability to change our circumstances is dependent on our ability to communicate effectively.
- It is preferable to control our physiology by breathing, moving, and touching techniques, rather than by resorting to pharmaceuticals.
- People who have a strong desire to improve social conditions so that they feel safer and can therefore prosper are called social activists.

Developing Our Understanding of Trauma

Van der Kolk's early studies played a significant role in rekindling debates over the effects of trauma.

Piere Janet is credited with discovering trauma and its relationship to psychological well-being in the late 1800s, according to legend. Janet is often regarded as one of the founding founders of psychology. He was also one of the first to recognize how past events in a person's life can contribute to present-day traumatic experiences. The phrases dissociation and subconscious were introduced by him, and they are still used today in discussions on trauma and traumatic experiences.

Van der Kolk recalls his early studies on veterans, which was published in the journal Veterans Affairs. Trauma, according to the results of Rorschach tests, can impair the brain's perceptions of reality. These exams played a crucial role in the way Van der Kolk approached his treatment sessions with survivors of incest later in his career. When he first started treating people, he did so through the lens of 'trauma.' Working with soldiers provided him with an appreciation for the extraordinary courage that trauma sufferers must muster to recall their experience.

Furthermore, Van der Kolk used this trauma lens to examine a broader range of individuals, demonstrating that trauma was far more ubiquitous than previously thought. Trauma can occur as a result of any event of great stress or agony that leaves the individual feeling helpless and hopeless.

Relationships Are Impacted By Trauma

Aside from the survivor, Van der Kolk noted that trauma has a considerable impact on those who are near the victim. Individuals who have experienced trauma frequently suffer from Post-Traumatic Stress Disorder (PTSD), which can lead to despair and substance abuse. Individuals who have experienced trauma may find it difficult to trust others. They believe that no one can comprehend what has occurred to them or why they are compelled to keep reliving it.

A group therapy session he performed for war veterans served as an illustration of this phenomena, as described by Van der Kolk in his writings. The program also assisted veterans in making new acquaintances with whom they could discuss their experiences. Those who had not been traumatized, on the other hand, were regarded as outsiders by those who had been. Because of this discrimination, Van der Kolk was regarded as an outsider by the traumatized group as well.

The only way to get through this obstacle was for Van der Kolk to put in weeks of listening, empathizing, and gaining trust. This anecdote demonstrates that we must first establish a connection with those who have been traumatized before we can expect them to trust us. Often, trauma is generated by those who should be trusted in the first place. As a result, it is critical to recognize that restoring trust might be challenging for traumatized individuals.

Trauma Can Be Treated With Therapy

Van der Kolk explained how the health of the brain and its adaptive responses to stressors are critical in the production of action. Consider the "fight or flight" reflexes that people have. Both of these situations necessitate taking action to relieve tension. When stress is severe, such as after a traumatic occurrence, problems can arise because the body's adaptive reaction is blocked, preventing the necessary action from being taken. In light of this, it becomes clear why eye movement desensitization and reprocessing (EMDR) is so important. This therapy assists the traumatized individual in learning to interpret information adaptively.

Brain Scans Recommend You Take Action

It is critical to address feelings of hopelessness or inertia as soon as possible. The feeling of hopelessness has been considered the most devastating aspect of trauma. Action is essential for healing because it disables the fight or flight survival system, which signals the body that it is safe. Because trauma can impair this survival reaction, our brain continues to generate stress hormones even though it has been stopped. Van der Kolk compares it to a smoke detector that is always activated. Consequently, even though you are not now under the influence of this stressor, your body is nevertheless behaving as if you were.

Stress hormones have a particularly negative impact on the brain because they reduce activity in a portion of the brain known as the prefrontal cortex. The prefrontal cortex is arguably the most important portion of the brain, as it is involved in every aspect of decision-making and planning.

As you are experiencing the trauma, the amygdala and limbic system are working at their utmost capacity.

This overload indicates that the region of the brain and the nervous system that is linked with emotions is constantly overactive.

A more accurate description of this reaction is "bottom-up" processing. Van der Kolk emphasizes that we should design therapies that support the recalibration of both 'top-down' and 'bottom-up' processing to better treat patients. The prefrontal cortex of the brain, which serves as a watchtower, should be better equipped to monitor the reactions of our bodies as a result.

The following are some strategies for improving top-down mental regulation:

- Yoga
- Mindfulness meditation

Recalibrating bottom-up mental regulation includes:

- Movement
- Breathing
- Touch

What Therapists Should Do When Treating Trauma

Mindfulness, yoga, breathing, movement, and touch are examples of top-down and bottom-up mental regulation techniques that can be used in trauma therapy. Trauma is defined by dissociation, which occurs when traumatic events disrupt our daily life. Here's a quick rundown of how therapists should approach trauma treatment:

(1) Assist in restoring a feeling of self in the physical body to clients. Mindfulness can assist in accomplishing this goal.

(2) Encourage the client to befriend, rather than suppress, body responses by drawing out any suppressed sensory information.

(3) Complete the self-preserving bodily activities that were hindered when the survivor was constrained or immobilized by terror and are now complete.

(4) Assist them in visualizing their situation. The fact that we have dreams demonstrates that our brain does not distinguish between real life and imagination. This suggests that imagination is critical in the healing process of the traumatized.

Neuroanatomy Is Altered By Early Trauma

Self-regulation is taught to children by their early caregivers through the use of mirror neurons, empathy, and imitative behavior. Early trauma alters the way the brain is wired, and neither medications nor conventional therapy can reverse these alterations in the brain's structure.

Van der Kolk cites his studies to demonstrate that trauma is the root cause of the vast majority of children's mental health problems.

Unfortunately, despite this, Van der Kolk was unsuccessful in his attempt to have the diagnosis of child developmental trauma disorder added to the Diagnostic and Statistical Manual of Mental Disorders (DSM-5) (Diagnostic Statistical Manual of Mental Disorders). The inclusion of this diagnosis as a replacement for the vast majority of pediatric diagnoses was his goal.

In his explanation, Van der Kolk points to the DSM's significant monetary value as the reason for its rejection.

Diagnoses should lead to actions, not the other way around. He claims that our present child diagnoses depict behavioral and emotional disorders that are the outcome of traumatic events in their lives.

Memories Of Traumatic Events Are Disorganized

Both healthy and traumatized brains store views of experience in neural networks but in different ways. Having said that, the most significant distinction between them is their level of arousal. Charcot and Pierre Janet were the first to describe post-traumatic stress disorder (PTSD) as a condition marked by acute emotional arousal.

Freud also gave talking remedies that were based on an energy reaction that was tied to a memory, with the resolution being to release or sever the connection that was making the reaction. Van der Kolk said that this type of dissociation entails distancing oneself from memory and the emotional connection that it has with it.

Specifically, Van der Kolk explains that research has shown that the organization of good and traumatic memories differs. Positive memories contain three distinct parts: the beginning, the middle, and the finish. Traumatic memories are disordered and fragmented, and they manifest themselves in the form of images, physical sensations, and emotional feelings.

Francine Shapiro, a psychologist from the United States, believed that unprocessed memories were at the root of many diseases. These memories inhibit our brain from changing our neural circuits in a more adaptable way.

As a result of advances in neuroscience and knowledge of how our brains can be modified, there is enormous optimism for our abilities to assist others in achieving and maintaining mental health and well-being shortly.

Bring Your Rational And Emotional Brains Back In Balance

The following are some of the recommendations made by Van der Kolk for effective trauma therapy:

- Find a way to maintain your composure at all times. Acquire the ability to retain your calm and attention even when you are provoked by old thoughts or emotions.
- Acquire the ability to be present at the moment. Maintain a sense of connection with others and with the present moment.
- Make an effort, to be honest with yourself. Maintaining your

integrity also means being honest about how you managed to withstand the experience.

Summary: Restoring the equilibrium between both the rational (prefrontal cortex) and emotional (amygdala) regions of the brain is critical to overcoming trauma. To control hyperarousal, you should practice breathing methods (also known as breathwork), cultivate mindfulness to increase your self-awareness, and establish solid interpersonal connections with others to move forward in your rehabilitation.

Apart from this fundamental base, Van der Kolk offers a plethora of treatment choices, including the following:

- Neurofeedback
- Theater
- Dance
- Yoga
- Schwartz's Internal Family Systems
- Movement
- Pesso PBSP psychomotor therapy
- EMDR

Mindfulness

Mindfulness has a comparable potential for allowing traumatized individuals to get in touch with their feelings. Mindfulness' major purpose is to help people retain conscious awareness of their bodies and emotions rather than denying them.

Trauma is typically accompanied by denial of feelings as a strategy of repressing uncomfortable memories. This denial inhibits wounded persons from commencing the healing process.

Mindfulness has consistently proven able to reduce some of the psychological and physiological impacts of trauma. Research also suggests that mindfulness can strengthen biological immune responses and stimulate the parts of the brain that govern emotions.

Yoga

Yoga is a highly effective trauma therapy. The body and the mind have a close relationship, says Van der Kolk. To live a balanced life, it is important to understand how your emotions affect your body.

Trauma can make this interaction between your body and mind particularly challenging to understand. For example, traumatized persons have a hypersensitive alarm system.

To handle this gap between body and mind, post-traumatic persons will turn to things that will dull their feelings. But this tends to inflict more harm than good. An alternative that seeks to help you come in touch with your emotions is yoga.

Van der Kolk explains that he has seen numerous patients successfully encourage messages about their emotional condition by using yoga. Yoga helps traumatized individuals to adopt stereotypically vulnerable positions inside a protected atmosphere.

Treat Trauma Like Any Other Experience

There are distinct differences in how we remember traumatic and non-traumatic memories. Sensory and emotional fragments play a large role in traumatic memories. This is because the shock of traumatic events overwhelms our brains, causing us to struggle to process all of the information.

Trying to remember the details of these experiences is an important part of overcoming trauma. If a person can process this information, they will be better equipped to put in place the structures needed to begin healing from trauma.

Conclusion

In the book, the author provides a brief overview of how our bodies and minds interact. The strong connection between trauma and our bodies is the subject of Van Der Kolk's research, diagnosis, and treatment of PTSD.

Drugs are generally thought to be the answer to traumatic experiences. However, he challenges this view. Alternatives include better understanding how trauma affects our minds and bodies and changing the way we process this information.

Printed in Great Britain
by Amazon

81647127R00031